Mark Blackburn

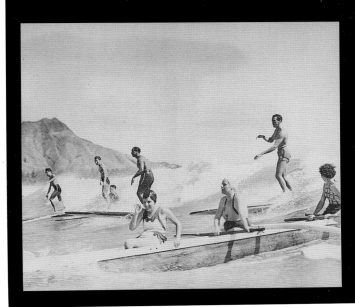

Hula Girls
& Surfer Boys
1870-1940

Hula Girls & Surfer Boys

1870-1940

Mark Blackburn

Schiffer Publishing Ltd

4880 Lower Valley Road, Atglen, PA 19310 USA

This book is dedicated to
Jeff and Jennifer Hyman
who in real life and spirit are
the essence of the Hula girls
and Surfer boys of the past.
With our warmest Aloha,
Mark, Carolyn and Kuhane
Blackburn.

Copyright © 2000 by Mark Blackburn
Library of Congress Catalog Card Number: 99-66042

Design by Blair R.C. Loughrey
Type set in Zurich/Swiss 721

ISBN: 0-7643-1042-9
Printed in China

Published by Schiffer Publishing Ltd.
4880 Lower Valley Road
Atglen, PA 19310
Phone: (610) 593-1777; Fax: (610) 593-2002
E-mail: Schifferbk@aol.com
Please visit our web site catalog at
www.schifferbooks.com
Please write for a free catalog.
This book may be purchased from the
publisher.
Please include $3.95 for shipping.

In Europe, Schiffer books are distributed by
Bushwood Books
6 Marksbury Rd.
Kew Gardens
Surrey TW9 4JF England
Phone: 44 (0)208 392-8585; Fax: 44 (0)208 392-9876
E-mail: Bushwd@aol.com

Please try your bookstore first.
We are interested in hearing from authors
with book ideas on related subjects.

When you hear the word Hawai`i, one of the first things that comes to mind for most people is the image of Hula girls and Surfer boys. It is with this concept that this image-driven book has come forth. For the last twenty or so years I have collected and put aside the items portrayed in this book as if this book was always in my mind. The concept for this book came up very quickly at a picnic with Peter and Nancy Schiffer on the DuPont Estate in Wilmington, Delaware, and the very next morning I went through my collection and realized that this book essentially was there in my drawers just waiting to be compiled. It was as if it had always been planned and in the works – a rather strange and serendipitous situation indeed!

In the last twenty years I have handled, bought and sold thousands of vintage images from all over Hawai`i and Polynesia but have always been fascinated with the subjects in this book, the result being that I have kept the most interesting and rare images. Why Hula girls and Surfer boys? I guess even in my own collecting habits these powerful portrayals from the past always represented to me the quintessential Hawaiian experience.

The history of Hula in Hawai`i is an ancient one with the tradition deeply rooted in legend and myth. From the time of Western contact with the arrival of Captain James Cook to the present, this art form has fascinated visitors to the Islands. It was with the arrival of the first New England-based missionaries in 1820 that this integral part and fabric of traditional Hawaiian society was frowned upon and discouraged only to make a revival under the last reigning King of Hawai`i, David Kalakaua. It was King Kalakaua, known as the "Merry Monarch," who single-handedly brought the Hula back to its former glory in the 1880s, encouraging its rebirth and revitalization. With the ensuing tourism that started in the 20th century, Hula became an exportable commodity of popular culture with many dancers traveling to other areas of the world, especially during the vaudeville era of the teens and 1920s. With the onset of World War II, Hula *was* Hawai`i with servicemen sending Hula dolls and postcards back to their sweethearts. Today, Hula is a powerful force in Hawaiian culture with competitions being held throughout the state, culminating in the world-famous Merry Monarch Hula Festival held once a year in Hilo, Hawai`i.

Hawaii.

COPYRIGHTED 1893 ARBUCKLE BROS

Known as the sport of Hawai`i's Kings, surfing's history is an ancient one deeply rooted, like Hula, in traditional myth and culture. Surfboards were highly prized by ancient Hawaiians, being passed down from one generation to another. The exhilaration of sliding down a breaking wave on a speeding surfboard was first described for the West by Captain Cook and other early visitors who were captivated by this previously unknown ocean sport. George Freeth, an Irish-Hawaiian, is credited with bringing surfing to America in 1907. Known as the best surfer in Waikiki, he went to California demonstrating his talents. It was Duke Kahanamoku, though, who brought surfing to the world and popularized the sport with his presence and notoriety achieved from his win in swimming in the 1912 Stockholm Olympics. Learning to surf at age eight, he was a natural in the water, spending his entire life involved in one way or another with the sport — the quintessential waterman of all time. With the rapidly increasing rate of tourism in the 1920s, Waikiki Beach became the center and cradle of surfing with the visitor, or "Malahini," trying his or her turn at the sport. The Duke and Waikiki beachboys of the Hui Nalu club were only too willing to help, and the sport received worldwide attention with returning visitors relaying their experiences on the waves of Waikiki. Surfing's post-war growth started in earnest with Californians like Tom Blake and Sam Reid traveling to Hawai`i in the 1920s. Such journeys were few compared to the influx starting after World War II and continuing to this day, with the sport rapidly growing and evolving worldwide. Today, as Fred Hemmings stated, "The soul of surfing is Hawaiian." I hope you enjoy the images in this book as much as I have enjoyed collecting them.

Aloha,
Mark Blackburn
Hilo, Hawai`i, 1999

White capped waves, billowy waves,
Waves that break into a heap,
  waves that break and spread.
The surf rises above them all,
The rough surf of the island,
The Great surf that pounds and thrashes,
The foamy surf of Hikiau.
It is the sea on which to surf at noon,
The sea that washes the pebbles and
  corals ashore.

from *The Surf Chant of* Naihe,
Chief of Kau
(translated by Mary Pukui)

Below
Houla-Houla girls, Chase photo, 1875.

Right
Hulahula or dancing girls, H. L. Chase, Cosmopolitan Photographic Gallery, 64 and 66 Fort St., Honolulu, H. I.

Below right
Heula dancers

Houla-Houla girls

Heula dancers

Henry Chase   HONOLULU H.I.

Henry Chase   HONOLULU H.I.

9 NATIVE WITH SURF BOARD, HONOLULU, H. I.

11 SURF BOAT OF THE NATIVE, HONOLULU, H. I.　　　DAVEY PHOTO. CO., H. I.

1336. Hula Dancing Girl, a Native of the Hawaiian Islands.

Circa 1900

It was performed by a circle of girls with no raiment on them to speak of, who went through an infinite variety of motions and figures without prompting, and yet so true was their 'time,' and in such perfect concert did they move that when they were placed in a straight line, hands, arms, bodies, limbs, and heads waved, swayed, gesticulated, bowed, stooped, whirled, squirmed, twisted and undulated as if they were part and parcel of a single individual; and it was difficult to believe they were not moved in a body by some exquisite piece of mechanism.

Mark Twain, 1872

HULA DANCERS.

(Honolulu)

Hulo hulo dancers

or

Hawaiian dancing girls.

Left
Chase photo, 1875

Above
"Huo hulo dancers or Hawaiian dancing girls."

Right:
"Hawaiians In Holiday Dress."
Merritt Gaunt (photographer?)

13 SURF BOAT OF THE NATIVE, HONOLULU, H. I.   DAVEY PHOTO. CO., H. I.

her angle of inclination became more critical, things began to look serious. The men were still bent over their paddles trying to achieve a speed as close as possible to that of the wave. In theory, this would have enabled them to shoot out ahead and to steer to the edge of the wave, away from the inevitable white water.

John Kelly, 1936

562   LAUNCHING THE SURF BOAT, HONOLULU, H. I.   DAVEY PHOTO CO. H. I.

Honolulu

Honolulu

454 HULA GIRL, HONOLULU, H. I.   DAVEY PHOTO

24

Left
Postcard, Copyright 1908 by Franz Huld Company, New York.

Top right
Private Mailing Card, Authorized May 19, 1898.

Bottom right
Private Mailing Card Published by the Island Curio Co., Honolulu.

16   ON THE BEACH OF WAIKIKI

Native with Swimming Board. Hawaii.

95. Famous Surf Riders. Hawaiian Islands.

HAWAIIAN HULA DANCERS.

Top two
Private Mailing Cards

Left
Hawaiian Postal Card,
Hawaiian Hula Dancers,
Feb. 1906.

No. 20. *Hula Dances in Full Costume.* HAWAIIAN SCENIC PHOTOS.
King Bros.,   ·Honolulu, H. I.

"Honolulian Young Ladies in their native rig-out, bedecked in floral attire according to ye custome! Hawain [sic] Islands, February, 1899, A W Cohen."

Hula Hula Singers & Dancers.

Hawaii c. 1895.

33

282 HULA DANCERS, HONOLULU, H. I.   DAVEY PHOTO. CO., H. I.

424 HULA DANCERS, HONOLULU, H. I.   DAVEY PHOTO CO., H. I.

35

Diamond Head and Surf Board Riding, Honolulu, T.H.

Surf-Board-Riding Waikiki — Honolulu.

Aloha Nui FROM HAWAIIAN ISLANDS

May 5 '09

Post Card. "Surf board riding is one of the great sports. The men made out as far as possible with the board that is shaped something like an Ironing board. Then they throw it on an incoming wave and on it they ride in shore. Some experts stand on their boards and balance themselves perfectly."

Post Card, No. 177 Hawaii & South Seas Curio Co., Honolulu, 1909.

151 Surf Board Rider. Hawaiian Islands

Private Mailing Card. Published by the Island Curio Co., Jas. Steiner, Honolulu.

101. Surf Board Rider. Hawaiian Islands.

Private Mailing Card. Published by the Island Curio Co., Jas. Steiner, Honolulu.

Surf-Board Riding, Honolulu

Surf Riding — Hawaii

Surf-Riding at Waikiki Beach, Honolulu, T. H.

"How would you like to try this - The boys paddle way out to where the big swells are - & come in like the wind standing up. It is the most thrilling graceful thing to watch and I imagine wildlly exciting to do - Wish you were all here to try it and also to eat the delicious pineapples and other fruits. Much love to you all. Charlotte Mack -"

Post Card 7608 - Pub. by Rose & Morris, Honolulu, T. H.

Hula Dancers, Honolulu

Aloha Nui

FROM HAWAIIAN ISLANDS

59 — Hawaii & South S as Curio Co., Honolulu. (Dresden, Germany)

A HAWAIIAN BELLE

SERIES C. OUR COLONIES

NO. 6. HULA-HULA DANCING FESTIVAL, HAWAII.

COPYRIGHT, 1903, BY W.R. HEARST.   COMPLIMENTS OF N.Y. SUNDAY AMERICAN & JOURNAL.

You can't imagine what you're feeling blue about. You simply glide and take a slide and you want to shout. You wiggle, you giggle, you wiggle to the Hula Blues.

"Hula Blues"
Song, 1911

H-23   Hula Girls, Hawaiian Islands.

Left
Post Card 40 - Hawaii & South Seas Curio Co., Honolulu, postmarked April 17, 1900.

Center
Carte Postale. No. 2552 The Hawaiian Islands. "Hula-Hula" Dancing Women, Published by Karl Lewis, Photographer, No. 136-D, Honmura Road, Yokohama.

Right
Carte Postale. No. 2553 The Hawaiian Islands. "Hula-Hula" Dancing Women, Published by Karl Lewis, Photographer, No. 136-D, Honmura Road, Yokohama.

Post Card postmarked Nov. 3, 1908.

You'll never know Hawaii 'til you've felt the foaming surf about your knees; 'Til you've plunged into the breakers with a cry of pagan glee.

Don Blanding, 1928

PUBLISHED BY THE ISLAND CURIO STORE HONOLULU

Greetings from
HAWAIIAN
ISLANDS

18. Surf Riding in Hawaiian Canoe at Waikiki.

Private
Mailing
Card

Post Card No. 25
Publ. by G. J.
Boisse, Honolulu,
T. H.

SURF BOATING AND RIDING AT WAIKIKI, HONOLULU

6212   Hawaiian Sailing Canoe

Post Card

"Arrived. Honolulu. - 14 days from Nagasaki. This is a beautiful place. Best."

Post Card No. 3514 Published by Cardelli-Vincent Co., San Francisco-Los Angeles. Postmarked Dec. 7, 1909.

Post Card

Post Card No. 77, Wall, Nichols & Co., Ltd., Publishers, Honolulu.

...a coral reef, against which the ocean is always breaking with a moan, as if it were weary of its long endeavor to destroy the barrier.

William Root Bliss, 1873

U. S. ARMY SOLDIERS IN HAWAII ENJOY SURFING, KING OF HAWAIIAN SPORTS

Surf Boat Riding, Waikiki, Honolulu

Post Card postmarked 1909.

18. Surf Riding in Hawaiian Canoe at Waikiki.

68. Surf Riding Hawaiian Canoe Waikiki, Honolulu.

Top two
Private Mailing Cards

Right
Post card postmarked
Jul. 21, 1908.

Surf Riding, Waikiki, Honolulu.

"This is lots of fun but sometimes they upset. I was upset in one the other day & got my foot pretty badly cut. L. S. A."

My Honolulu Girl.

62 HAWAIIAN GIRL

PUBLISHED BY THE ISLAND CURIO STORE HONOLULU

Left
Post Card postmarked
May 18, 1909.

Center
Private Mailing Card

Right
Private Mailing Card
postmarked Nov. 17, 1906.

61 HAWAIIAN HULA DANCER

PUBLISHED BY THE ISLAND CURIO STORE HONOLULU

"The decorations for the "original" hula dance consisted only of a grass skirt very much abbreviated. Robert."

The Island Curio Co James Steiner, Honolulu, Hawaiian Islands.

Native Musicians, Hawaii, Playing "The Star Spangled Banner."

Post Card copyrighted 1908
by Franz Huld Company,
Publishers, N. Y.

II.   Native Hula Dancers, Hawaii.

PUBLISHED BY ART LITHO. CO. SAN FRANCISCO FOR WALL, NICHOLS CO LTD HONOLULU

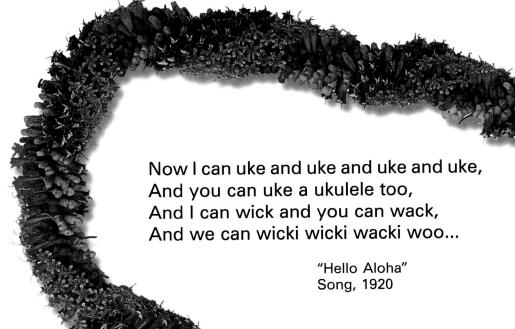

Now I can uke and uke and uke and uke,
And you can uke a ukulele too,
And I can wick and you can wack,
And we can wicki wicki wacki woo...

"Hello Aloha"
Song, 1920

168 Hula-Hula Dancer, Hawaiian Islands.

Hawaiian Beauty.

Hula Dancers,
Hawaiian Islands.

Post Card pub. Exclusively for The
Island Curio Co., Honolulu, T. H.

25

THE CAPTIVATING HULA

If you never saw the hula,
I'll show it now to you:
I give a little wiggle and a little twist or two,
An undulating motion with my body and my hand;
That's how we dance the hula in Fair Hawaii land!

Private Mailing Card
Published by the
Island Curio Co., Jas.
Steiner, Honolulu.

Aloha Nui

HAWAIIAN
HULA GIRLS,
HONOLULU.

Three Post Cards, Sydney Short Line, Nineteen Days.

I love a pretty little Honolulu *hula hula* girl,
She's the candy kid to wriggle,
Hula girl
She will surely make you giggle,
Hula girl
With her naughty little wiggle...

"Honolulu Hula Girl"
Song, 1917

*"A fairly typical
Hawaiian girl with
her ukelele.
G. H. Barton"*

*"Wouldn't you like to be
me and have one with
you all the time."*

Post Card postmarked May 1 (year indistinct).

HULA
GIRL

Sea of the striking of the big wave
The foam of the waves of Hiki-au
Sea of surfing a noontime

Ancient Hawaiian Chant

Post Cards

The Surf-Rider
HAWAII

Surf Board.
Waikiki.

Left
Post Card from Hawaii Promotion
Committee, Honolulu, Hawaii.

Center
Post Card Hawaii, from Hawaii Promotion
Committee, Honolulu, Hawaii.

Right (front & back)
Post Card with sticker for Matson Line to
Hawaii, One sailing each week from San
Francisco, Service to the volcano direct.

Chewing tobacco premium, 1913, Duke Kahanamoku...World's Champion Athletes free with Pan Handle Scrap

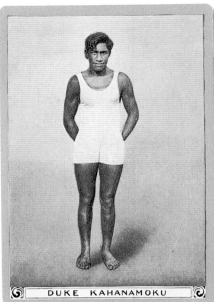

DUKE KAHANAMOKU

Post Card showing Duke Kahanamoku

DUKE KAHANAMOKU

Duke Kahanamoku, who broke all records at the swimming contest in the Stockholm Olympic, is a Hawaiian, and, like all his countrymen, has been used to the water almost from his very birth. Caucasians have little chance against the Hawaiians. This native holds the 50- and 100-yard records in Hawaii, and is credited with having made the century in $54^{4}/_{5}$ seconds, or $1/_{5}$ second better than by Cecil Haley, of Australia, made. In February, 1911, at Pittsburgh, he made 50 yards in $23^{4}/_{5}$ seconds and 100 in $56^{1}/_{5}$. He made 100 feet in a tank in $14^{1}/_{5}$ seconds, beating the record. His best time for 100 yards in fresh water was $55^{2}/_{5}$ seconds. In the tryout before leaving for Stockholm he made 220 yards, with one turn, in 2 minutes, 40 seconds. At the Olympic he won his heat in the semifinals, 100 meters, in 1 minute $2^{2}/_{5}$ seconds, and the final heat in the race in $1:3^{2}/_{5}$. At Hamburg, a few days later, he still further lowered the world's record to $1:1^{1}/_{2}$.

WORLD'S CHAMPION ATHLETES
FREE WITH
PAN HANDLE SCRAP

WE HONESTLY BELIEVE WE HAVE PRODUCED IN PAN HANDLE SCRAP THE FINEST CHEW THAT HAS EVER BEEN OFFERED.

FACTORY NO. 6—FIRST DIST. OHIO.

14

DUKE KAHAMENOKU
CHAMPION LONG DISTANCE SWIMMER

Premium card for Wilbur Chocolate Company, 1925, "Duke Kahanamoku Champion Long Distance Swimmer."

I watch a hula dance last night
Upon a beach of sand so white
Its crescent reproduced the moon.
The surf with driving crash and swoon
Set up a rhythm in my blood.
Kukui torches cast a flood
Of murkey orange light that played
About the dancers as they swayed.

Don Blanding, 1923

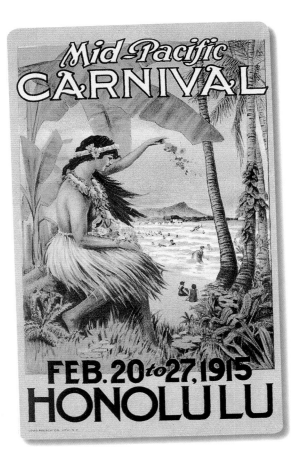

Post Cards showing the progression of a hula dance.

"See Naples and die"
—They spell it differently here:
See Hawaii and live.

Jack London, 1916

ee the **FAMOUS**
AWAIIAM HULA DANCE
BY THE BEST HAWAIIAN HULA PES.

LAHAINA MAUI T. H.

Maui, T. H., 1925"

Princess Kaminini - Hula Dancer
Honolulu. T.H.

"1927"

Post Cards, one postmarked 1917.

The water that rolls in on Waikiki Beach is just the same as the water that laves the shores of all the Hawaiian Islands; and in ways, especially from the swimmer's standpoint, it is wonderful water. It is cool enough to be comfortable, while it is warm enough to permit a swimmer to stay in all day without experiencing a chill. Under the sun or the stars, at high noon or at midnight, in midwinter or in midsummer, it does not matter when, it is always the same temperature—not too warm, not too cold, just right. It is wonderful water, salt as old as ocean itself, pure and crystal-clear.

Jack London, 1911

THE OUTRIGGER GIRL
PHOTO BY BAKER HONOLULU

"Miss Hoapili, English-Chinese Hawaiian"

A Honolulu Maid
Baker Photo

"Dearest, Aunt Hester saw these babies do the
native dance and play the uekele (sic). See
you soon love.   Aunt Hester"

Advertising
stamp, 1920

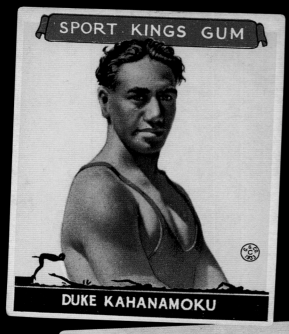

—No. 20 —

DUKE KAHANAMOKU
(SWIMMING)

The world's record books of a few years ago, are filled with new marks established by Duke Kahanamoku. Greatest and most famous of all swimmers developed in the Hawaiian Islands, Duke safely holds his title as Sports King with his remarkable performances which mark him as the greatest all-round swimmer of all time. A great racer, an expert diver, a star performer on the surf-board and a marvelous water polo player, Duke leads them all. Traveled in many countries and established world's records in the 50 and 100 yards, 100 metres, 150 yards, and longer distances, both in open water and in tanks. In 1912, he thrilled spectators at Olympic Meet in Stockholm with a new record for the 100 metres, free style, in 1 minute 2-2/5ths seconds. That year was crowned World's and Olympic Sprint Champion. Turned professional in 1917.

This is one of a series of noted athletes and sportsmen. The complete series includes all the leaders in every branch of sport. START YOUR COLLECTION NOW.

SPORT KINGS CHEWING GUM
THE GOUDEY GUM CO. BOSTON
Made by the originators of
INDIAN and BIG LEAGUE GUM

Premium card No. 20 Duke
Kahanamoku (swimming) for
Sport Kings chewing gum, 1933

Post Card, "Surf Board Riders,
Honolulu, Swimmers par excellence"

Post Card postmarked Mar 18, 1910. "Surf bathers Waikiki beach Honolulu."

Surf bathers
Waikiki beach Honolulu

The swell which rolls over the reef comes up gently to the edge of the shore...A bath in this summer sea is delightful. The water is very buoyant, clear and pleasantly warm, its temperature being about seventy degrees. Once in, I am reluctant to leave it. But can we not come again tomorrow?

William Root Bliss, 1873

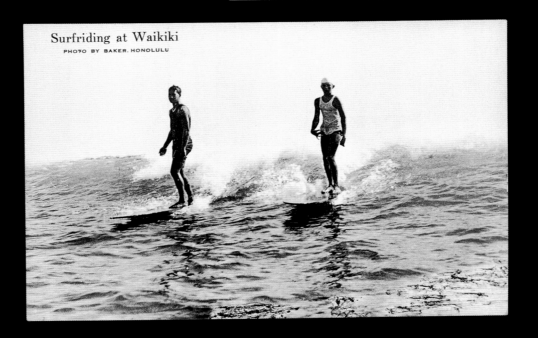

Surfriding at Waikiki
PHOTO BY BAKER. HONOLULU

Photograph copyright 1925

Outrigger Canoe

Post Card, Surf Riding at Waikiki, Honolulu

Post Card, Photo by Baker, Honolulu

Post Card, Photo by Baker, Honolulu

82

Surf Board Riding, Hawaii.

Post Card Published exclusively by The Paradise Postcard Co., Honolulu. Surfriding is justly called "The King of Sports" for these is nothing to compare with it in all the world; that rush shoreward on a surfboard at express speed, ever in front of a huge white-capped billow, provides those fortunate enough to experience it with sufficient thrills to last a lifetime.

Surf Riding at Waikiki, Honolulu

Premium card, Sports of the Centuries (A Series of 25) No. 15 Hawaii... for Dickson Orde & Co. Ltd. Farnham : Surrey : England

Post Card, copyright 1916

Post Card, received May 4, 1921.

"Best regards From Honolulu Hawaii James Miller. (reverse) The picture was taken by Mr. Baker a photographer whom I got acquainted with some time ago and is sold thru out Honolulu. I thought that I would send you one and see how you would like it Jimmy Miller From Honolulu Hawaii."

Post Card A Maid of Honolulu,
Photo by Baker Honolulu.

SURF RIDING, HAWAII.

Surf Riding, Honolulu, T. H.

Surfriding at Waikiki.

Top left
Post Card 14 Published by Hawaii and South Seas Curio Co., Honolulu.

Top right
Post Card 46 Published by M. H. Weinberg, Honolulu, T. H.

Right
Post Card Published exclusively by The Paradise Postcard Co., Honolulu, H. T.

SURF-BOARD RIDING. WAIKIKI. HONOLULU

SURF RIDERS, HAWAII.

"Just imagine spending Xmas and New Years in the tropics- and being in swimming! But the surf is glorious. These islands are so beautiful that I frequently shed tears! Queer isn't it, but I can't help it. Best wishes for pleasant Xmas & New Year & all other times from- Casey"

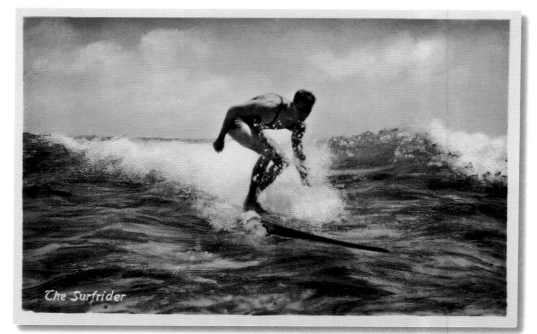

The Surfrider

Each (surfer)...would paddle three or four hundred yards out to sea, (taking a short board with him), then face the shore and wait for a particularly prodigious billow to come along; at the right moment he would fling his board upon its foamy crest and himself upon the board, and here he would come whizzing by like a bombshell! It did not seem that a lightning express train could shoot along at a more hair-lifting speed. I tried surf-bathing once, subsequently, but made a failure of it. I got the board placed right, and at the right moment, too; but missed the connection myself. The board struck the shore in three quarters of a second, without any cargo, and I struck the bottom about the same time, with a couple of barrels of water in me.

Mark Twain, 1872

2. SURF-BOARD RIDERS OF HAWAII—THE SPORT OF KINGS!
Oceanic S. S. Co's splendid 16,000 ton, twin screw steamers sails every 21 days.

OCEANIC S. S. CO., LINE TO HAWAII, SAMOA AND AUSTRALIA

SURF RIDING AT WAIKIKI.
PHOTO BY BAKER HONOLULU

Surf Riding at Waikiki, Honolulu

Real Stuff

A Maid of Honolulu

PHOTO BY BAKER HONOLULU

Post Card Published
by the Paradise
Postcard Co.,
Honolulu, H. T.

Surfriding at Waikiki.

"It doesn't look so but here the waves are like mountains."

Surf-Board-Riding — Waikiki — Honolulu.

PUBLISHED BY WALL NICHOLS COMPANY LTD. HONOLULU

31   CANOE SURF RIDING, HONOLULU, T H

Post Card Pub. exclusively for The
Island Curio Co., Honolulu, T. H.

Sport in the Surf, Honolulu, T. H.

Post Card T. Chrome.
No. 7, Wall, Nichols &
Co., Ltd., Publishers,
Honolulu.

Natives surfing, Honolulu, T. H.

Surf Riding - Waikiki

Post Card received May 4, 1921.

Post Card postmarked May 21, 1926.

"Elule, Kauai. Got here well and had a pleasant trip, will be leaving on the 7 of June. Been here already 3 weeks hoping you are well. With best regards from Kathrine and my self."

Post Card, "Hula dancer on board U.S.S. New York Sept. 23, 1920 T. Hawaii.

A Maid of Honolulu
PHOTO BY BAKER HONOLULU

"My dear Bertha, Just a line to say I am getting along fine. I hope this letter find you in the best of health and happy. Your Friend Dan"

Sea Gods

Gods of the surf in mad excited race
    Speed to the shore with shouts of lusty glee;
Swift as the wind their wild exultant pace
    Riding the white-maned stallions of the sea.

Left
Duke Kahanamoku in the surf.

Two at right
Print and poem by Don Blanding

Victorious

Hand Colored Post Card HA-11 Hula Girls in Honolulu, in ti-leaf skirts and leis.

H - 288 Hilo Hattie

When Hilo Hattie does the Hilo Hop,
There's not a bit of use for a traffic cop-
For everything and everybody comes to a stop,
When Hilo Hattie does the Hilo Hop.

Now when Hattie does her stuff, they cry for more,
And everybody knows what they're crying for.
The sailors leave the ships at sea and swim ashore,
When Hilo Hattie does the Hilo Hop.

Now when Hattie *oni-onis*, there's no doubt
That's she's a girl who knows what it's all about.
Babies hush, women blush, strong men passout,
When Hilo Hattie does the Hilo Hop.

Song, 1930s

108

1919 - Hawaiian Blossoms and
Flowers on the Lawn of the
Volcano House, Kilauha, T.O.H.

Post Card S-648 - Hula Girls and Canoe
- Hawaiian Islands, postmarked Jan 18,
1944. "The only place you see them is
in a picture. Tom White Jr. "

Post Card, Hawaiian girl
on board (Honolulu)

Photography by Billy Howell at Don
Beachcomber's on the beach at Waikiki, 1931.

#30 HULA MAIDS

Top left
Photo Post Card, Entertainers - Kona Inn. "1- Movie of Mauna Loa eruption shown here. 2- Grass circular rug unique. 3- Outdoor dances in front of grass hut."

Top right
Post Card 666 Holoku Hula - Hawaiian Islands

Left
Post Card postmarked Dec 9, 1940. "Dear Gang! Having a wonderful time. Sure wish you were all here. We leave for Manila, P.I. this evening - Merry Xmas "Lee"."